Romancing
the Sur

Romancing the Sur

Reflections on Life in Big Sur

Linda Sonrisa Jones

Copyright page:

Published by Survision.

For a gallery of images, visit survision.org.

Author photo by Caitlin Reclusado, recklessarts.com.

To learn more about the non-profit organizations that support the Big Sur community visit bigsurfire.org, bigsurhealthcenter.org, big-surgrange.org and henrymiller.org.

Big Wheel is a trademark of Louis Marx and Co., Inc.
Greyhound is a trademark of Greyhound Lines, Inc.
Miata is a registered trademark of Mazda Motor Corporation.
Scrabble is a trademark of Hasbro.
Tang is a brand owned by Mondelēz International.
Wellington is a registered trademark of Hunter Boot Limited.

ISBN: 0692884769
ISBN 13: 9780692884768

Dedication—

To my Mom, who introduced me to the wonderful power of words.

Grant us help then.
Help us to be more of the Earth each day!
Help us to be
more the sacred foam
more the swish of the wave!

—PABLO NERUDA

Contents

Romancing the Sur

Like a mighty sailing ship of centuries past, Big Sur is a she. We stand on the prow of her highest cliff and look back to see the curves of her landscape.

Steep ridges of forest and grassland slope down to the sea like thighs opening to incoming tides. Ridgetop swales are tummies soaking up the sun; swelling hills are high round hips and dimpled bums.

Loving this compelling, dangerous and beautiful Big Sur isn't easy. She's captivating and she's worth it, but sometimes we wonder.

She's fickle, and when she does treat us right, there is no guarantee that her love will last. She demands real-world sacrifices, which we make year after year before we see the consequences of our choices. She's touchy, and sometimes harsh, as anyone will say who's felt the sting of local gossip, or paid the price for a wrong move, especially on the road.

When we're cold and out of firewood, she doesn't care. When we're lonely and far from friends, she laughs. We distract ourselves from our struggles as she dishes out her own dramas, oblivious to ours.

We grow older in the comfort of her company, yet remain wary of her next move. She's a powerful observer who comes to know us very well. Ultimately tender, when we die she takes us home.

When she reveals herself, it's only in those moments when we are authentically open to her charms. She surprises us as we come around a curve on the highway. There she is, veils of mist swirling up to her sturdy knees, those classic cliffs plunging into the sea and receding down the coast, so beautiful that we just want to cry.

She seduces with the lightest touch—a moment of eloquent stillness in the morning. She soothes us with her seashell pink dawns and coral sunset skies. Always changing, she teases us with her great majesty, plays hard to get with her astonishing beauty.

Now we see her; now, as we focus on our own limited lives, we don't.

She is queen of the sounds of silence: serenading frogs, whispering owls, rumbling surf, moaning trees, wingbeats. Most of all, she is a great teacher, probably more teacher than lover, really. When she gives of herself it is when we are ready, when we have done our work—when we have shared our joys, and pursued our passions.

Wildfires, storms, and mudslides contrast with gentle days that we wish could last forever. The sea sparkles with diamonds, birdsong ripples through the forest, and the sunset glows on the horizon. We soak in an existential solitude that heals our souls.

The lunar goddess makes her home in Big Sur, too. She rises full above the ridgetop, a redwood tree silhouetted against her bone-white orb. She spills her vivid light down canyons onto the expansive ocean, and we are transformed.

A Teabag Steeped in God

There is a tradition in Big Sur of bathing out-doors, preferably in a claw-foot tub. We soak, we groom, we contemplate the view in a magical brew of exotic oils and scented soaps. We let the amniotic waters take us in completely. Perhaps a humming-bird sips nectar from an aloe or sage blossom just inches away from the edge of the bath.

Admittedly, we might not be as perky as we should be as we begin our workday. But the sensuous af-terglow of an early-morning outdoor soak is worth it. Just have that extra cup of java, take some deep breaths, and quietly file away the sensations of a deli-cious tryst with the tub.

Some time back, I was perplexed by a percussive sound I heard coming from the tub. Ping, ping, ping. What was it? Upon investigation, I discovered acorns, falling rhythmically from a nearby oak, landing against the cold white porcelain. Fluttering birdsong, the wind through the leaves, and ping! ping! filling the tub with the makings of acorn mush.

Who else takes their binoculars into the bathtub but Big Sur folks? Watching whales, dolphins, condors, and hawks while bathing creates a sense of wonder. Once, I heard the heavy wingbeats of a condor above me, the sound of an angel in flight.

Sometimes, though, the majestic vista is just too much. Instead, I watch tiny birds at the feeder, or bees on the flowers.

You could say that I live in Big Sur because of a bathtub.

I was on a wild weekend trip with an outlaw boyfriend. We ended up on a mountain south of Nacimiento Road, in a tub clinging to the slope of a forested canyon. While soaking amidst the warm bubbles, I remember nibbling on mint leaves growing beside the bath. I felt a whisper of fate, and knew I would return.

Many years later, after a Dionysian Christmas celebration, my neighbor and I strolled outside to stargaze. Two ladies tipsy on champagne, we riffed on how living here saturates us in nature.

As we looked at the full moon riding low in the night sky above the sea, we coined a phrase that says it all: "I feel like a tea-bag steeped in God!" *Yes.*

Here, it's not "Let us pray," but instead, "Let us steep." The mystics say God is everywhere. So let us steep deeply in God, in a bathtub in Big Sur.

Samsara Perfume

Big Sur serves up fire like no place else on Earth. There's an epic grandeur to the destruction, framed against ocean, mountains, and sky.

Of all possible soul-twisting life events, fire comes near the top of the list. Forest fires on this scale make clear that we are a microscopic part of the cosmos.

Many of us have learned through fire that great loss and radical changes of perspective go hand in hand. Sometimes those shifts come as a whisper, other times they're more like a shout. The gifts fire brings are always profound.

The Pfeiffer Fire, erupting at midnight on a late December evening, proved that life turns on a dime. Those who happened to be awake at that hour saved several lives. They smelled smoke, saw flames, and went door-to-door yelling to their neighbors to run for their lives. People fled with the clothes on their backs and nothing else. Thirty-foot flames in gardens and beside cabin windows led to emergency convoys over back roads, down the mountain to safety.

First came the call, announcing the danger. "There's a fire, a fire: we're leaving now!" I walked down to the point below my home to see. I thought my neighbors had left their lights on, but then, those lights were an infernal red. I walked further and saw an enormous cauldron of vivid flames boiling over the mountains ten miles to the north.

So many acres, so many homes, so many people displaced: disasters are always reported with numbers, as if the numbers can help us to digest the event and somehow convey the power of the story. Those of us who live with the reality of losing, almost losing, or fighting to save our homes, know that integrating fire into personal experience takes the tincture of time.

And then, the soul gifts arrive, just in time for Christmas.

We are connected. None of us is really alone. The Pfeiffer Fire produced an outpouring of support and donations within our community and beyond. Also, we are more resilient than we realize. I think of my friend who fought the fire for hours in her flip-flops (and probably could have done it in her high heels.)

We are not our stuff. What an amazing feeling it is to walk away from a lifetime of belongings and know that we'll really miss only one or two—or maybe, three or four—things. What we miss takes on a special significance: a favorite painting, a silk robe, a teapot. Losses like these are offset by the fact that we, and our loved ones, are alive.

Renewal and rebirth really happen. As hard as it may be to believe at first, bit by bit we come back to ourselves. Fire transforms us into something brighter and stronger, adamantine. Many of us become gypsies during fires, and recreate our lives from that simplified perspective.

Shortly after my thirtieth birthday my little in-law apartment in the Oakland Hills burned to the ground, part of an urban firestorm that claimed three thousand homes and twenty-five lives. For a time afterwards I lived in a state of grace, where everything seemed to glow with an inner, pulsing light.

I had just started learning about Buddhism, so the concepts of nirvana and samsara were fresh in my mind.

Everything I looked at I saw simultaneously whole and exploded into ash. One afternoon I found myself fascinated by the contents of the medicine cabinet in my friend's 1940s-era apartment. As I peeked behind the mirrored door, one item jumped out at me from the middle shelf—a small perfume bottle labeled in blood-red letters: *Samsara*. Samsara, the turning wheel of existence, the world of suffering and desire.

When our awareness is forever altered, when our sense of complacency and safety is destroyed, it is a ripe time for learning new things, for greater clarity, for healing. From destruction comes creation, the eternal law. We are all of us fire gypsies, floating with the flames.

Wish and Blow

Perhaps you too remember this: making a wish by blowing on a delicate globe of dandelion seeds? It was a summer custom as I grew up, my breath propelling the tiny white parachutes, watching them float onto lawns and flowerbeds. My wish would come true if all the seeds achieved liftoff at once, launching themselves into a new life.

If you live with a serious gardener, such practices are discouraged, since re-seeding a weed is not really recommended. But still, each summer here in Big Sur, I find many opportunities to wish and blow.

Last week I noticed a perfect specimen as I drove down the dirt road from my home to the highway. For days, this promise of a plant, with its crown of woven white seeds, stood unwavering beside the flow of trucks and cars bouncing up and down the ridge.

Like blowing out candles on a birthday cake, there is a metaphor in the ritual of scattering seeds via breath, a hopeful way of letting go. Seems we are always blowing our way into the next moment, moving towards what we wish for. We know that the shore we reach, the lawn or flowerbed we land in, will most likely bring us something different from our dreams, and yet be exactly what we need.

And, musing on the wisdom of seeds and what they have represented to humans over millennia, I come across the words of Hafez, the fourteenth-century Persian poet:

> Light
> will someday split you open
> even if your life is now a cage . . .
> for a divine seed, the crown of destiny,
> is hidden and sown on an ancient, fertile plain
> you hold the title to . . .
> From a sacred crevice in your body
> a bow rises each night
> and shoots your soul into God.

Brave Music of the Distant Drum

O the brave music of the distant drum!
—OMAR KHAYYAM

A few years into my adventure in Big Sur I accepted an unforeseen responsibility: helping an older gentleman to live independently on the ridge.

Due to turn ninety in February 2008, Bob Nash lives in a simple two-room shack on the forest's edge. After serving in World War II in the Aleutian Islands, Bob came here in 1951. He'd spent some time in Berkeley with the Beats, then bicycled down the coast to Big Sur. During his first years here he served his time, as we say, in tents and platforms under the redwoods.

Bob first saw the notorious author Henry Miller in the Pfeiffer Big Sur State Park. Miller drove past him in his lime-green Cadillac as Bob sat on a bench with his lady companion. She said reverently, "That's Henry Miller!" Bob eventually met Miller through (surprise!) a woman they both were courting.

Bob became a regular at Miller's dinner parties, quietly observing the intellectual, bohemian world that Miller enjoyed. The talk around the table was of art, current events, politics and philosophy. Miller himself was reserved, perhaps saving his commentary for his writing.

During this time Bob heard the call to become an artist as well.

His passionate output consists of tens of thousands of works—unique and mysterious line drawings. Evocative and tiny, approximately two-by-two inches, the drawings depict the elemental world in its most ephemeral qualities. Created with india ink and fountain pens, Bob once described a drawing as inspired by the flight path of a yellow butterfly.

Miller nicknamed Bob's drawings "visual poems," and wrote of them in his essay *Journey to an Antique*

Land. This was the introduction to Bob's autobiography, *On My Way.* Now out of print, this slight but profound tome relates Bob's life story.

His background is pure Americana. His father was an Episcopalian reverend in the Wyoming wilderness. One of Bob's favorite stories is of how, as a young boy, he met a bishop of the Episcopal Church who told a story of Chief Joseph, also known as In-nut-too-yah-lat-lat (Thunder coming up over the land from the water.)

Bob says:

> I was born in Jackson Hole, Wyoming, in 1918. When I was a young child my mother heard of a retired Episcopalian Bishop of the Territory of Wyoming (prior to statehood in 1890) who would conduct a sermon in Kelly, a small town ten or fifteen miles north of Jackson Hole.
>
> We went, and I remember nothing of the service, but afterwards there were maybe a dozen people standing around and I was introduced to the old gentleman. What a wonderful face he had! He must have been in his

late eighties, close to my age now, come to think of it.

A woman behind me, who I never did see, with great awe in her voice, asked, "Bishop, did you know Chief Joseph?" The old man's face lit up with a wonderful smile, he threw up his hands and laughed. "Oh yes," he said, "I knew Chief Joseph for more than thirty years. He was the holiest man I ever met, and I could not convert him."

That scene has been with me for over seventy years. I take it as reminder that there are many roads to the ultimate mystery of life.

There you have it, straight from the genuine, accept-no-substitutes Old Man on the Mountain!

Bob's home is decorated in an eclectic mishmash of wooden tables, dust-covered books, piles of clothes, and Christmas lights that twinkle all year round. His desk, also his dining table, has a stack of music in the corner next to the radio, a few photos of friends, bills, silverware, and a random jar of maraschino cherries next to the peanut butter.

As I've fussed with the clutter over the years, dusting, hanging pictures and paper lanterns, finding him colorful, cozy bed linens since he's now spending more time reclining, I've noticed the emergence of many shades of pink in Bob's home. A beautiful actress in a movie poster wears bubblegum pink lipstick; a ceramic hand holds a fuchsia feather boa. In a large framed print from a visiting photographer, Bob wears a coral-colored plastic lei.

I once asked Bob what people did in Big Sur before modern technology arrived. No internet, no cell phones, no satellite TV, not even radio for many years. "Did you watch the grass grow?" I joked. Bob replied that he embarked on a study of learning Mandarin Chinese from a textbook, and added, "There was always ice cream."

In 1969, Bob married Rosa Marchesano Nash, a former nun from the Immaculate Heart of Mary. Rosa met Bob during a retreat on the ridge, and they began a correspondence. After receiving dispensation from the Vatican to marry Bob, she joined him here and they built a little cabin together.

Bob worked as a handyman on the ridge, while Rosa became a much-loved tutor to local children.

Together, they tended roses in their small garden and crafted the rustic ceramic plates, bowls and religious icons prized by many of us today.

A little over a decade ago Bob suffered the loss of Rosa, then quite suddenly, he developed macular degeneration and had to give up driving. Now he relies on the assistance of his neighbors and friends.

He reports that the key to his success as an elder is having younger friends with "flexible" minds, who share new ideas with him and help keep him flexible, too. A steady flow of pilgrims comes to his door, and to all his visitors he dispenses wisdom, tells stories, and listens intently to tall tales.

Like many older people, Bob loves young children, especially feisty little girls. Twenty some years ago he was a surrogate Grandpa to a brilliant child who grew up on the ridge. Framed photos of young Heidi peek out from Bob's desk and walls, and she is all smiles.

Bob's secret is that he is both physically and psychologically strong. How else could he live in an uninsulated shack without a bathroom and cook on a hot plate for decades, his only entertainment a radio, books, and an assortment of visitors? He engages with life in his own special way. He finds people fascinating, especially, as he says, those of the "female variety."

His tremendous empathy, his feeling for the pulse of the land and of the people and animals he loves, seems a great triumph to me.

When we're young, naturally we're immortal; nothing can wound us permanently, or stop our momentum. It's only later that we begin to get a glimmer of our looming "extinction," as Bob says.

Now in antiquity, Bob's death holds him close, watching over him, visible in his unsteady hands and trembling breath, the beginning of a curtain call. To see this is terrifying and awe inspiring. To live with it each day and night as he does is unimaginable to me.

He still devotedly markets his artwork. Many times he has told me that he is worth millions and plans to buy me a solid gold Cadillac someday. Yet his line drawings are quite obscure. Over the years many devoted fans have attempted to launch his works into the larger art world. I tell Bob that his art includes his successful bohemian on-a-shoestring life here on the mountain.

The sunset tonight is a bright orange splash at the horizon, topped by a cover of slate-blue cloud. We watch as it all turns into a tide of magenta. Bob has spent so much of his life right here, witnessing this stupendous display. I ask him about all this sunset watching, and he acknowledges this luxury with a nod of his head. "And the mornings," he adds, in a solemn tone.

Another part of Bob's secret is his ability to do nothing, to simply be. This skill is so odd nowadays it's practically subversive. I tell him, "No one lives like this anymore, Bob, unless they're a monk in a temple!" He smiles up at me from his chair and says, "But I am."

The thoughtful soul to solitude retires.
—Omar Khayyam

Heidi's letter

Dear Bob,

I've been having dreams about Big Sur again lately. And woven into these lucid tapestries are images of you. When I awake, I sift through the pictures and attempt to decipher the facts from fiction. Sometimes memories of a place grow wings . . . while deep in slumber it seems perfectly logical for a dirt road in Big Sur to lead to a cathedral in the English countryside.

In my dream I could only see my hands, smaller and caked with clay, pointing upwards, begging you to tip that rose, the big red one, down for me so that I might smell it. You are in an orange down vest, letting out a gentle laugh. Always willing to indulge my six-year-old demands, you guide the heavy blossom near my nose. I can still smell the tart sweetness of the sun-warmed roses in your front yard.

Memories of you, and that once-upon-a-time life, also conjure up the smell of freshly rained-upon oak leaves—such a unique, earthy scent. I remember kicking up leaves while hunting for chanterelles below your house, the cuffs of my jeans wet from the tall grass. I think to be a kid in Big Sur is heaven.

My mind floods with memories. A red swing that used to hang near the dome, the lower pond where I would catch pollywogs, the fairy tree, the spot where the red hen always hid her eggs, the tall grass Max and I would fashion into straws with which to sip Tang on hot summer days.

The smell of fresh hay in the goat house, the strawberry patch below the big house, the buzz of hungry bees beneath the grape arbor, the little creek that in winter flows with what I called coffee water. The venerable old avocado tree that Gramma would hang a radio in blaring KGO to scare away the raccoons. My favorite yellow rose bush that I will some-day buy and plant when I have found my own home. The images are rich and vivid, yet some were formed before I knew words and I find it impossible to translate them onto paper.

Well, I wanted to drop you a note to let you know that I was thinking of you, and this re-minded me of a million beautiful things I thought I had forgotten. I hope this finds you happy, healthy, and warm. Maybe on my next visit to Big Sur we can have tea. Thank you for everything.

Love,
Heidi
(printed with permission of Heidi Sutton)

Church of the Convertible

In the Church of the Convertible prayers are always answered, sometimes in surprising ways. A matador-red Miata landed on my doorstep last month, and when I take this pretty pony out for a spin everything is beautiful again.

Many of us in midlife find ourselves seeking answers that soothe, enlighten, and heal. As I wake up with quicksand in my bones and my brain becomes more porous every day, I ask: How much playtime do I have left? Has it all been worth it so far? And, most ominously, what do I do now?

Perhaps it's time to renew my love of play and pleasure, knowing that life is not forever, and that this really does apply to me. Voilá: the midlife crisis!

Sometimes, it's OK to live a cliché—to take up flamenco dancing, and fall in love with a car.

In Spanish, the word for convertible is *descapotable* (des-cap-oh-tah-blay). Such a sexy word, conjuring Hemingway, bullfights, and love in the afternoon.

As I downshift into the tight curves of our American Riviera in Big Sur, hairstyle-protecting scarf in place, I remember Grace Kelly in *To Catch a Thief,* and try not to think about her demise.

With Kipling my dog riding shotgun, my needs are wonderfully clear: the car I've waited thirty years to drive, my dog as my co-pilot. There is therapy in simple pleasures, after all.

Most of the wild men I've known drove sporty cars, so I confess to that psychic imprint of fast cars = sexy. As advertising firms know well, there *is* something sexy about a driving experience that demands complete presence, and fills drivers with a feeling of immortality.

Sportscar driving is really an awareness practice. We are not going from A to B in some quiet behemoth that feels more like a living room than a car, playing a video game with our lives. Rather we are *driving* with precision, and a higher level of consciousness. With all the traveling I do in Big Sur and out into world, it's a thrill to be just inches above the pavement, paying close attention.

I've no desire to talk on the phone (can't hear) eat (doesn't really work) or apply makeup (can't shift gears with lipstick in my hand). I'm hyper-aware of my speed, other drivers, and the natural world around me, especially with the top down! This lovely loaner Miata has a Momo steering wheel. As my mechanic said with awe, "It's a *performance* steering wheel."

Last weekend I drove through the highway corridor of towering eucalyptus trees near San Juan Bautista, made famous in Hitchcock's *Vertigo*. Shadows of these sentinels fell across the lanes in the late afternoon sunshine. When I entered the Big Sur Valley sometime later, I imagined the bird's eye view of myself from the tops of the redwoods, a hawk or crow's vision captivated by a low roar and a flash of red.

The sound of the engine, the feel of the wind, the smile on my face. It's funny how life is more beautiful when you're awake. Like Cinderella at the end of the ball, soon I will return this scarlet carriage to the fairy godfather who so kindly loaned it to me. But I have been reborn in my new faith, the Church of the Convertible, and will worship as often as I can!

Big Sur Bee-tox

Well, I know how it happened, and it's quite dramatic. A wee bee, furious and scared, got trapped under the bill of my baseball cap. We mutually freaked out—I batted her away while she swiftly stung me and presumably died. The poison entered the soft flesh on the point of my cheekbone, a finger's breadth away from my right eye.

I turned and ran back down the mountain, cutting short my before-dinner walk with my dog. My face hurt, and I had a sense of dread about what would happen, but I didn't see any sense in getting emotional yet. It was a beautiful evening, and I'd just had another Big Sur experience. It couldn't be as bad as a rattlesnake's bite, or a scorpion's kiss.

When I reached home I realized the stinger was hanging off my cheekbone, so I carefully extracted it with a pair of tweezers. Then we carried on entertaining our guest, eating pasta, drinking champagne, and reading Tarot cards. As the evening wore on, our dinner guest commented on the transformation of my face. "I think it's not going to get any worse," he said. "I think it's as swollen as it will get." Not a very encouraging thing to hear.

All night long I put baking soda compresses under my right eye, watching the poison spread across my face. My left eye swelled up too, and my cheeks inflated. In the morning I wore a scarf to partially cover my face and went to work, thinking this would take my mind off the pain. An hour later I went to the local health center instead. The country doctor there gave me a steroid shot and assured me I'd be better soon.

Back at home I sank into the grass, ignoring the bees dancing around me. I let the blessed sun warm my body while I held an ice pack across my face. Leftover codeine tablets and some homeopathic anti-anxiety drops calmed me down somewhat. The drops are "Buddhism in a bottle," promising to reduce anxiety, stop nervous irritability and obsessive thinking. I should probably buy a barrel of it.

Still, the really massive swelling had yet to occur, turning my face into a mask with swollen eyelids and a pink puffy smile. As I looked at myself I thought that maybe, just maybe, I could banish vanity from my life, at least a little.

This is when I turned into a venerable Tibetan lady, one who'd spent her life tending yaks in the winds of the Himalayas.

A friend stopped by and was properly horrified. "I hope you get your face back soon," she said. So did I.

Yet here's the silver lining: I had been standing on the edge of the pool, gazing into the daunting world of "women of a certain age"—pricey creams, floppy hats, and always turning my face away from the sun. What happens to all faces eventually was suddenly not such a big deal anymore.

I suppose I have to thank that tiny distressed bee, who accidentally gave up her life, for helping me to renew my dedication to growing old *gracefully*.

Today, I touch the spot on the tip of my cheekbone where the stinger left its poison. It is still there, the littlest bump. I hope it stays. It reminds me that bee-tox *is* better than botox, and to be grateful for the face I have, which, thank goodness, came back.

It's Three O'clock in the Morning

It's three o'clock in the morning, and my world is about to change, forever.

It's a hot summer night. The dry, heavy air is thick with chirping crickets. Stars twinkle in the sky above, and a corridor of light from the planet Venus shines across the sea, from the horizon directly to my door. Earlier in the evening I'd lit a few candles, burned piñon incense, danced, and prayed.

At 3:00 a.m., I'm still so uncomfortable and hot that I decide to venture forth to the outdoor bed to gaze at the billions of stars in the Milky Way. I'd lost my temper with my rickety screen door earlier, so it sat outside on the lawn. I'd left the sliding door to my bedroom open as I fell asleep, the better to hear the cricket choir.

As I get up to go out, stuffed bunny, pillow, and blanket under my arm, I notice my Siamese cat, Minnie, peering at my altar, a low table beside my bed covered with flowers, candles, and icons.

I bend down to see Minnie's view, thinking I'll find a frightened mouse, or maybe a bat curled up on the table. But no. What I see is a full-grown, blotchy-brown sleeping rattlesnake, coiled up around my sculpture of the Egyptian Goddess Hathor.

What follows is a blur, even to me now, years later. I am still recovering from this event. I race to the phone and call my closest neighbor, Jim, and leave him an abject message. In the kitchen I grab a pair of long barbecue tongs, and hear the pioneer woman voice in my head: "Come on, sugar pie, woman up!"

When I go back into my bedroom, tongs in hand, Minnie prepares to take a swipe at the reptile. I scream, and guess what? The snake emits a low, ominous buzz. That does it. I run out of the house into the warm night . . . to meet Jim, shirtless, in blue jeans, dashing down the path to help me. We collapse together, hugging. My head tucked under his arm, pressed against his skin for a moment, I hear his heart beating, fast.

"What is a rattlesnake doing in your bedroom?" he asks me. Then he answers, "Well, I guess a rattlesnake goes wherever it wants to!"

"Let's get Emmett," we say together. "He has guns!" So we do.

We stumble down the path to Emmett's tiny cabin. He's our local cowboy and neighborhood elder statesman. He's shared many stories with us of his adventures with dangerous beasts.

Emmett is sitting up on his cot, wide awake, clearly happy to see me in my pink sleep shirt and green Wellington boots. "Well, hello," he smiles at me, flashing his broken teeth.

"We have a situation," I announce. As I tell him the details, his eyes get large and he picks up a machete from beside his door and hands it to Jim. I had forgotten: Emmett is terrified of rattlers.

"Oh no, Mister Snake Whisperer, you're coming with us!" I say. With great calm he pulls a loaded hand-gun out of the pocket of his work jacket. "That'll do!" I say.

Jim—machete in hand—and I hurry back to my bedroom door, hoping that the snake is still on my altar and not roaming about the house. It's gone back to its nap. I have a moment of sadness for this monster who picked the wrong place to spend the night.

Emmett appears in full military camouflage gear. He stands in my bedroom and points his gun at the altar.

"Cover your ears," Jim says, and we stand outside in the cool grass and watch Emmett fire several shots. Pop. Pop. Pop. Pop. Pop. Bright sparks of gunfire in my bedroom. There's no hissing or rattling so I assume he's got it. Later, I'll find a bullet hole in my altar, a memento of the evening.

"Did you get it?" I ask.
"Well . . . uh . . . no," he answers.
"What?" Jim and I shout in response.

He begins to poke at baskets under the table with his walking stick. "Ah, I hit it," he says, and as I return to the room I see a few drops of rattlesnake blood leading, dear God, behind my bed. Had it been there before?

It's a captain's bed, so Jim and Emmett pull back the mattress and Emmett fires a few more shots at the snake, huddled on the carpet, trapped between drawers. Finally, it's over.

After administering the mercy blow with the machete, Emmett tosses the limp serpent onto the barbeque grill outside, and closes the lid. Safe at last, we stand together in a moment of silence.

As we stumble back into the kitchen I say, "This is bad, but, uh, I could *really* use a drink!"

Jim points without hesitation to the top shelf of my kitchen cabinet. "You've got some Jack Daniels there." So we open it, and drink a few shots together. I learn that Emmett loved being christened the Snake Whisperer. Jim jokes about how I have called forth numerous rattlesnakes over the years, though this is the first one to slither into my bedroom. Am I doing snake dances here or what?

"These are the times," Emmett says as he pours himself another tumbler of the golden liquid. The laughter and stories begin to flow, and I realize how right he is.

As we decompress and share what's up in each of our worlds, I'm aware that these two crazy guys are really my family now. Family shows up when you're freaked out, takes care of you when you're in danger, and laughs with you to bring you back to more ordinary reality.

Later, I dance alone by candlelight as the pale dawn seeps into the house. Still wearing my gardening boots and sleep shirt, I stomp out a special dance for my altar-snake.

Between stomps I repeat aloud, "This is it!" over and over, not knowing why. Primal energy pulses through me. It will be a week before I can sleep in my bedroom again.

The next day, I ask my shaman friend what this episode could possibly *mean*.

She looks at me with her serious dark eyes, pauses for a long moment, and says, "I think it means . . .

you should keep your screen door closed at night."
After laughing her wise-woman laugh, she adds,
"That lady snake sacrificed herself so that you can
become more awake to necessary transformation in
your life."

After that night, big transformation turned out to
be barreling towards us all: Less than a year later,
Jim was dead from cancer, my marriage was dissolving, and Emmett had lost his marbles, threatening
another neighbor with his shotgun.

We all sensed that our gathering that evening
marked a once-in-a-lifetime Big Sur event. But how
could we know that our adrenalin-fueled, wee-hours
party, hunting down a rattlesnake and celebrating
after, would become our last crusade together?

Man from Another Time

When I described my neighbor Jim, I often said, "He's like a man from another time."

Today, I would say he's a bodhisattva. In the days after his death, I heard Jim's sadness in the raven that cried for hours outside my window. Now, in the mornings I hear Jim's joy in the finches singing in the treetops, songbirds that can't be seen but whose music we hear all around. Like them, Jim will always be with us here on the mountain.

Some esoteric teachings hold that the soul incarnates every 140 years. So I wonder: will Pink Floyd be around 100 years from now, when Jim comes back? I know he would like that.

Why is it that when someone dies, we are always left longing for more essential contact with them? Jim didn't tell us how bad his cancer was. I imagine he downplayed the gravity of his condition so he could enjoy the love and optimism we gave him in those last, too short, weeks.

In Big Sur we treasure our privacy, nurturing ourselves with nature's vistas, both expansive and intimate. Many of us also share the wonder of our gardens with loving friends. Jim did this, and for years much laughter and joy flowed from the little house on the edge of the cliff where he lived.

Jim was a genius, a trained engineer, but decided he didn't want to be part of the corporate world, choosing a free-spirited life instead. With his gentle laugh, perfect olive skin, and 70s rock star hair, he could have had a career in the music industry, a wife and kids, a house in the hills. But he chose instead epic sunsets, sports on the big-screen TV with his friends, and a little dog named Vinnie.

The range and depth of Jim's musical knowledge, his love of sound, was profound. He was the audio guru for musical events here in Big Sur, and was able to do the work he loved at the Monterey Jazz Festival for many years.

"Sit here," he said, directing me to a space on the well-worn black leather couch in his living room. "This is the sweet spot for hearing sound," he added, putting an album on the turntable. Sound waves from the huge speakers and the old-fashioned amplifier made my body vibrate to Pink Floyd's classic "Shine on you Crazy Diamond." "Welcome to the Church of Analog," he smiled.

Jim died the way no vital, well-loved, and hardworking person should die in this country—uninsured.

The night before he left us we discussed his application for Obamacare insurance coverage. He had taken some pain medication, and was indulging in the company of a lovely young woman. His energy was bittersweet—sad and overwhelmed but also happy to be enjoying the evening.

It is heartbreaking to tell someone you love that they're "going to be OK," while desperately hoping that you're right.

Jim fell asleep on his couch that Tuesday night in December, and slept all night long, a rare release from his pain. In the morning he was still dreaming peacefully as the cancer flowed over his body like a dark tide. In solitude on the mountain he loved, he slipped away.

There are those who said that, given the kind of cancer he had, his peaceful death was a blessing. But Jim was not ready to die, and would not consider his death, at 47, just a few days before his mother came to visit him, as any kind of blessing.

The gentle guest who joined us for years of dinner parties and holiday celebrations, always late, with a big smile on his face and a nice bottle of wine under his arm, will no longer shine with us on this mortal stage.

A noted old-timer has said, "I couldn't imagine a heaven more beautiful than Big Sur." There is comfort in knowing that Jim lived his dream here for several glowing years. We pray that he is now at peace, serenely tuning his guitar in heaven, surrounded by celestial sound.

The Wedding Tree

Everyone needs a magic charm, and here's mine: I have a very feminine tree that I like to hug. It comforts me to tuck my head against her trunk thighs and look up and down the coast. It feels like I'm peeking out at the world from behind Mama's skirts.

This small oak grows on the point below my home, on a finger of land forming the side of one of the ridge's small canyons. Slightly pruned into a trim shape, she's occasionally festooned with prayer flags and serves as a witness to the words of lovers. She shelters sunset watchers and wandering poets, and appears in mystical landscape paintings.

Big Sur's mountain ridges spread away from her to the north and south, so her backdrop is the ever-changing ocean and sky. From under her branches,

I sometimes feel a shiver of vertigo, as if I were a red tail hawk swooping down towards the sea.

Probably the most interesting and most commented-on aspect of the Wedding Tree is that if you look at her with soft eyes, you will see that she is in fact a woman. Her torso is plunged into the earth, while her two sturdy legs reach up towards her dancing branches. She has an upside down "muffin top," a serious belly button and a dimpled behind. The question is, is she diving down into the earth, or emerging up out of it?

Maybe she's doing handsprings, leaping from ridgetop to ridgetop down the ages. Perhaps she's an Esselen tribal princess, transformed into an oak in some ancient, indigenous fairy tale. Either way, she is our tree goddess.

One morning last week I woke up like the rest of the world. After listening to city sounds in my bed, I drank a cup of coffee in my friend's kitchen. Then I walked out onto the street, got into my car, and drove to an office building, where I talked about the business world all day.

How blessed I felt the very next morning when, wearing only my bathrobe, cowboy hat, and clogs, I played pied piper to my cats who followed me down the hillside. In this way I began my day, leaning against the Wedding Tree's warm tummy and soaking up the strength of her primeval thighs.

Here Come the Lupines

Today is the first day of spring, and every spring in Big Sur seems lovelier than the last. We've had gentle winter rains, and dreaded debris flows from summer forest fires did not flood the valley or close the road. The mysterious chanterelles have made a comeback appearance, peeking out from beneath the ash and oak leaves.

Now comes the time of the plumes of royal blue lupine and the golden cups of California poppies. They arrive along with the coral red tufts of the Indian paintbrush and the long-stemmed, pale-lavender blue dicks. This amusing name presumably comes from the Latin name *Dichelostemma multiflorum*.

Mother Nature is the most gifted florist, mixing wildflowers in delirium-inducing waves of color and scent. Smelling the fermenting soil and the sweetness of the ankle-deep lupine smeared across the mountain, I feel life coming up out of the earth here like nowhere else I know.

Imagine Gramma making lupine blossoms into preserves on a warm afternoon in her farmhouse kitchen, a soft breeze carrying the fruity grape-like aroma through the screen door. Something that smells so good must be tasty too—perhaps a lupine tart or sorbet would make an unforgettable dessert.

The spring after the 2008 fires produced an especially vibrant poppy bloom. Waves of saffron poppies splashed across mountaintops beside fields of royal-blue lupines. In forests and along roads, deep-purple wild lilacs contrasted with bright-yellow scotch broom.

My friend Marlene and I hiked to the top of the mountain with the goal of submerging ourselves in poppies. Yet, when we reached the golden meadow, we saw that rolling around in the flowers would trample their delicate beauty. So we reclined carefully instead, gazing from our bed of blooms down to the sea.

Marlene, a former Montessori teacher and PhD psychologist, sighed deeply and declared, "The poppies . . . are happy!"

Some years ago I rediscovered the children's story "The Selfish Giant," by Oscar Wilde. This inspired us to host an annual Easter-egg hunt here on the ridge. Every Easter Sunday dozens of local children search the garden, filling their baskets with candy-filled eggs, sparkly treasures, and chocolate treats hidden by the Easter Bunny.

"The Selfish Giant" teaches that spring really begins when forgiveness and love fill our hearts. This famous allegory of magical renewal and redemption is as tender as a bouquet of wild lupines, as uplifting as an extravagant Easter bonnet.

As a young girl, I learned that one should never pluck the Golden Poppy, the state flower of California. Here's a little poem that I often remember at this time of year—

I will be the gladdest thing under the sun.
I will see a thousand flowers and not pick one!
—Edna St. Vincent Millay

Stop, Look, Listen

At a certain point every spring, almost over-night, a tribe of yuccas come striding over the rocky slopes of Big Sur, all the way down to the sea.

A lifetime ago, on a birthday pilgrimage that turned into a back-roads adventure, I saw my first *Yucca whipplei*, known more romantically as Our Lord's Candle.

I had taken a detour on a faint broken line on my map. It turned into an endless, narrow dirt road over the mountains. Seeing no one after several switchbacks, I found myself headed east instead of west, and began to experience some serious pioneer angst.

Stepping out of my car on that summer day I stood dripping sweat in my sky-blue cotton sundress and shot a photo of the golden yucca growing out of the rock directly above me.

Photography places us firmly in the present and provided me that day with a moment of peace. In the process of focusing and creating art, we are briefly liberated from the chatter inside our heads. Tibetan Buddhists call this chatter *Sem,* the discursive mind.

In Big Sur there are many opportunities for liberation from monkey mind. There are fewer distractions, and we are often challenged by the elements. Because of this we live a little closer to the rhythms of life, and have a sharper sense of impermanence. Life is perhaps more of a Tibetan sand painting here, with equal parts beauty and vulnerability.

We watch the light change as the sun comes up, and watch it change again at the end of the day. We sit in front of a wood-burning stove in the mornings, listening to the soft hissing and popping of the fire. Or we stop to enjoy the wind as it blows around us on our walks, ruffling the trees, disturbing the birds.

Add to this the eternal, heart-stopping views of the ocean and mountains up and down the coast, the wholeness of nature and God, breathing deep all around us. To paraphrase Eckhart Tolle, when we fully experience beauty, the mind stops.

There are many time-honored ways to stop and feel that comforting place we all know inside that doesn't require the gob-smacking beauty that Big Sur provides. We can observe a flower open in a pot on a windowsill, light a candle, sip a cup of hot tea, or gaze quietly into the eyes of a beloved.

Pauses filled with stillness connect us with who we really are. My dream is to string these shining moments together, bright beads in a mala of time.

Sunkist

The kiss of the sun for pardon,
the song of the birds for mirth,
we are closer to God in a garden
than anyplace else on earth.
—Dorothy Frances Gurney

My Grandmother Olive carried this poem inside her all her life. It's one of the first verses I remember learning, and it returns to me often, especially on a beautiful spring morning when I'm looking forward to getting my hands into the dirt.

Gramma introduced me to the fairy-festival scent of sweet peas that climbed up a high fence in her garden. There was the dark mystery of the moist African violets on her kitchen windowsill. From her I learned how to choose the most promising baby plants at the nursery, and how to grow geraniums from cuttings—just stick them into the soil, add water and wait.

As I write this I watch a hummingbird drink from the furry red kangaroo paw blossoms that hang over the deck beside my bedroom. The hummer's throat feathers flash magenta in the morning light. A little shot of bliss flows through me as I watch this simple dance of bird and flower.

The phrase "Ten minutes being present in nature is equivalent to a year in therapy" caught my ear this past week. This is the kind of spiritual longing I know well. To be healed of worry by the magic of sunlight, birdsong, an earth-scented breeze.

Perhaps it's not these experiences in and of themselves that heal, but our openness to the natural world that nurtures without fail. After years of living in Big Sur, I'm confident that this is the trick.

Without beauty of some kind, the soul shrivels. Of course, we suffer in Big Sur too, yet the landscape here has an immediate healing impact. If we step outside and take some deep breaths, go for a hike or watch a sunset, we feel immensely better.

A gift of geranium cuttings has inspired me to plant them beside my outdoor tub this morning. This way our guests will flavor their steaming baths with fragrant geraniums, as well as with the lavender and rosemary nearby. I'll plant the stems with the sweet-smelling leaves, their star-like shape repeated in a dark purple pattern in the veins of each leaf.

Then I will weed, because I promised I would. Soon my mushy, confused modern heart will be soothed by the love of our greatest mother. She is the one we can always turn to. She lives the deepest truths found inside the earth, the sky, the sea, and in each of us.

Report from the Front Lines

As I write this report, my beloved dog sits beside me in the corner booth at Fernwood, our local tavern. I've just seen an enormous plume of smoke above Mt. Manuel, behind Pfeiffer Big Sur State Park. The ridge I call home is under mandatory evacuation.

Mama Big Sur took the form of a towering cylindrical cloud on Summer Solstice day last week. An opening in the base of this thunderhead streamed bolts of lightning first into the ocean, and then onto the top of Grimes Canyon. Big Sur's notorious polarization of light and dark, of brilliant positive charge and violent destruction, combined to start the worst fire here in a century.

Earlier today my neighbor Sula encouraged me to make a run for it to my house from the valley, coaching me on how to talk my way past the sheriff's roadblock. "Don't be afraid, be clear and strong. And don't be coquettish," she admonished me in her proper British accent.

So at the roadblock, I tell the cop the truth: "My husband is fighting the fire. I'm going up there to get my dog."

"OK" he answers, and waves me on. Official permission is like a shot of adrenalin. I'm in for it now, I think.

Leaving the Big Sur Valley, I drive past Grimes Point, where the sheer rock face was dynamited to make the highway in the 1930s. Hot rocks, loosened from the burning brush above, fall on the road around me.

Up at the house I make a dash for the treasured items I've thought about—wedding dress, photo albums, laptop, and a few things guaranteed to comfort me—fluffy bathrobe, socks, love letters.

I work fast, and have time to say my prayers to Kwan Yin gazing peacefully over the pond, and Ganesh, perched sleepily by the bathtub. "Thank you, thank you, thank you, for my time here so far. I am grateful, so grateful."

Cold beer in hand, I collapse briefly in my blue wooden chair, and gaze down the green swale of grass to the sea. A breath, a sip, a moment. Then I hear the forest service truck arriving. With another handful of belongings I head towards my car, grabbing a souvenir baseball cap on the way out the door.

I hold the cap up to show my husband as he comes down the path in his volunteer firefighter's uniform. "Go Giants!" I deadpan, ashes falling around us.

I remember our neighbor, the elderly Bob Nash, who left us a few short months ago. Bob, the cosmic linchpin, lived here for over 50 years and was never touched this closely by fire. Today I see him as a wizard, long white hair streaming in the wind. He stands on the dirt road, arms upraised, commanding the blaze, "Thou shall not pass!"

Driving down the highway that evening, I see the unspeakable. Three giant watersheds, Grimes, Graves, and Castro, all on fire. Dark banners of smoke fan out from the top of each mountain, like three volcanoes in a row.

The air is hot and heavy with smoke. Even the shadows are still, as if the forest is watchful. The sky glows dark, filled with soot and tinged with pink. Firelight. The ocean is stone gray, reflecting this nightmare that is not a dream.

Fleeing the fire to join neighbors in the valley has its benefits: Time spent over meals, wine, and games. Conversations about what we treasure and what we fear, sharing prosaic and profound moments. We laugh, embrace, and comfort each other in authentic community.

How else would I know how my friends make their coffee in the morning? How they carefully sweep crumbs off the dining room table after dinner, and play card games with their children in the evening? How they darn socks in a rocking chair as they discuss the day, or take a nip of scotch in a crystal tumbler before bed?

These are things we discover when we spend time together, not entertaining, but just being. These windows of intimacy are priceless to me.

this time we sleep as much as we can, and savor bits of contentment like sucking free candies. Everything is in relief. I see things I don't usually see, and feel everything more intensely—the curly starfish on an altar, the soft sand around my ankles on the beach, endless restlessness in my body.

I think constantly of our homespun cathedral, sitting empty and quiet, the activity of each day turning peacefully around it, still safe from the flames.

What does the light in my bedroom look like now? Do the fruit trees need watering? Are the koi in the pond hungry? Is the rooster still crowing all day long after his release from the coop beside the forest? Is the crystal hanging in the window splashing rainbows across the living room?

"Welcome back to the fight." says Victor Laszlo to Rick in the final moments of *Casablanca*. "This time, I know we'll win." There is no greater love than to put your life on the line for a person, a cause, or a place. Here all three converge: a community of souls that are spiritually fed by reverence for this land. *Hiraeth,* the Welsh call it, a longing for the land.

A Public Service Message

Last Tuesday, "the man" and I had a little chat. Since there's no cell phone reception on ridgetop, when I get off the mountain and into cell range I make and receive numerous calls on my little red phone. I get very excited whenever it rings, and always answer calls. Which is what I did as I was waiting in the left turn lane, driving from Rio Road onto Highway One.

Whoops! Yes, that squad car is for me, I think, as I pull to the side of the highway near the picturesque fields stretching up and down the corridor of Carmel Valley.

"So," he says, blonde, attired in regulation khaki, holding his clipboard, his shadow falling across me. "Can you tell me why I stopped you?"

This is good, I think, as the wheels in my brain start turning, gauging the potential of clever banter with a man in uniform.

"Um, my car is really dirty?" I ask meekly, glancing at the layer of road dirt on my wagon's rear window. There's a distinctive fan of clear glass shaped by the wiper blade. Someone has drawn a peace sign in the dusty upper left-hand corner.

"Nope," he says, "try again."

"Uh, I didn't use my turn signal?" I look up at him and squeak this out.

"No," he says once more. "You were talking on your cell phone."

"I bought one of those expensive ear-thingies," I reply, "but I lost it."

"So, why don't you use your speakerphone?" Now, it's his turn to sound just a tiny bit pleading.

"I can't figure out where the button is," I admit.

He sighs. "License and registration, please." Dang. Then, I dive into the well of my passenger seat, digging about for my documents. As I do this I realize my backside is up in the air, giving the cop a good view. This seems to have no positive effect, either. Oh well.

"Why don't you have your registration in your glove box?" he asks. (Like you're supposed to, he implies.)

"My life is chaos!" I reply. My car sometimes serves as my suitcase, camping kit, and mobile office.

By now I have climbed into the back seat, still looking. I show him the dinosaur excavation kit I just purchased for my neighbor's ninth birthday. This gets a smile from him.

As he writes me up, outside, beside his squad car, I wonder how many locals are driving by, observing my misadventure. In fact, since this corner of Highway One is the beginning of the main artery all of us use to travel down the coast, my story, or a version of it, could make it back to Big Sur before I do.

And of course, the following afternoon a colleague asks me, "Hey, what was up with you and the Sheriff?"

I'd enjoyed heartfelt exchanges with all the people I'd met that day. The lady I bought coffee from in the café taught me how to say good morning in Turkish. The sad-faced grocery clerk and I chuckled over the horrors of holiday muzak. The man at the toy store told me he felt like Tom Hanks in the movie *Big*, and so on.

Perhaps, in my golden, happy-for-no-reason day, I was due for a friendly interaction with the law.

So, yes, it's dangerous to talk on your cell phone while driving. Accidents can and do happen as a result.

As our chat ends, Officer Dainty (I swear that's what his name looks like on my ticket) showed me where the speaker button is on *his* cell phone.

As I sheepishly returned to my dirty blue Subaru, parked beside the highway, Officer Dainty had one more thing to say. "And hey, clean your car!"

French Tea with the Empress

Sula Nichols lives on a historic ranch at the top of the ridge with her four children, three horses, a pony, and one very old dog. Also in residence are several cats that come and go, and a bearded dragon lizard.

Known whimsically to her friends as the Empress of the Universe, Sula comes from a family of extraordinary women. Like many charismatic people, she exerts a magnetic draw on kindred spirits. The Earth is the "opal of the universe," she says, and she is passionate about protecting our planet.

You can find Sula's profile on a classical Greek vase. Penelope perhaps; Artemis, absolutely. She is essentially mythological too; tall, statuesque, with golden-green eyes and a tumult of dark curls. She positively hums with breezy confidence and crazy wisdom.

Last Sunday I sat down with Sula for "French Tea" in the afternoon sunshine at her well-worn kitchen table. We shared a bottle of the widow Cliquot's champagne, and our conversation floated along on the effervescent bubbles. Later, we dined on a plate of savory pasta, plus crisp lettuce and juicy cherry tomatoes straight from her garden.

Sula's small, warm home overflows with pictures of her children, siblings, and self at various life stages. The walls hold a gallery of paintings she's created—portraits, sensual landscapes, and dancing horses.

Horse blankets, cowhides, a saddle, a piano, a white board listing to-do items, pots and pans, glassware, shoes, clothes, flower vases, and more are scattered everywhere. This is serious artistic clutter, adding to the mix four wild children and their mother's adventurous spirit, in spades.

Sula grew up in Hydra, Greece, and in Suffolk, England. At the age of ten, she developed a crush on an American GI stationed at a local NATO base.

She loved American movies (from *The Apartment* to *Easy Rider*) and of course, that great American export, rock and roll. She was drawn to the dream of the flower children in San Francisco and the possibility of an expansive bohemian life in a new world.

In 1977, she got her first taste of the American dream in New York City and Hollywood, then took a Greyhound bus from Santa Barbara to Monterey. Like many arriving in those days, she hitchhiked back down the coast to Big Sur.

It was overcast the afternoon that Sula's ride took her to Nepenthe, known as the "land of no sorrow." The restaurant terrace was bathed in golden light when she arrived, but the rest of the coast to the north and south was wrapped in heavy fog.

Like the parties on Hydra she remembered from childhood, locals danced their cares away at Nepenthe, almost every night. She met her friends there, and later that evening they drove to the ridge.

Then, Big Sur magic. Driving up from the fog blanket tucked in along the highway, a warm breeze welcomed them on the ridgetop, and the indigo sky shone with galaxies of stars. The next morning, Sula drank in the view of infinite sea and sky and vowed she would never leave.

I ask her what has sustained her during her decades on the coast.

The inability to take this place for granted. The weight of the continent, my love of the land. I've been to many beautiful places on the planet, but Big Sur remains the crown jewel. I can always pour whatever sadness I have into the ocean. She receives it, and gives me back a sense of calm, of happiness, of feeling complete.

I carry Big Sur inside myself now. It is the most powerful land, a polarizing touchstone, really. It's a place to ground and to release and receive energy. There are two opposing poles of energy here, in the mountains and the sea. These powers of positive and negative energy intensify each other, yet stay in balance. In these conditions, there can be no denial of absolutes.

In this vein of combining poetry and science, we discuss polarization and prisms. In prisms, the twist in the middle, where the light changes, is the most transformative point, where it's most alive.

So, the polarizing energy of Big Sur creates the possibility of intense change. If you have something in you, or something happens to you, it can be a blessing or a curse. Here in the land of no denial, you must go with it.

At twenty-one, Sula married, and welcomed her beautiful first-born daughter Sarah. She has raised four children in Big Sur, and gave birth to two of them on this mountain. They range in age now from thirteen to twenty-six. I'm curious about what effect Big Sur has had on her family's story.

"My children say it's marvelous to have a place in one's childhood that is magical," she says. "Big Sur is a beautiful 'point of departure' in that children learn how to be present in nature. But it's important not to get stuck here. Growing up here my daughter Sarah appreciated the horses. My son Torre has great friendships, while my twins Layla and Jasper connect more with the land."

My first vision of Sula's teenaged daughter Sarah was on a summer day. The air smelled of bay, eucalyptus, and the warm dirt of the road. I heard a rhythmic rustling of leaves in the forest, and looked up to see a maiden on horseback cantering up the path. Sunlight shone all around her as she smiled and waved. It was a scene from my imaginary childhood.

Later, Sarah tells me some of her own memories. "Calling out to my cousins who lived up the road with birdcalls. Riding down the hill in our Big Wheels, totally naked, using our bare feet for brakes. We did that as long as we fit on the bikes. Covering each other in mud and 'painting' designs on each other with pomegranate seeds. Oh, and riding bareback in the moonlight."

Sula and I laugh over a memory of Layla, at ten years old, playing in the waves at Pfeiffer Beach in the depths of December. She skipped through the bone-chilling surf draped in wide ribbons of bright-green kelp, wearing nothing but a Santa hat.

As Layla and Jasper come tumbling into the kitchen, Sula smiles. "Here come the children, my *terrible* children." Later, as we watch the sun sink gently into the Pacific, the Empress and I embrace in contented silence.

The Wingéd Life

He that binds to himself a Joy
does the Wingéd Life destroy.
He that kisses the Joy as it flies
lives in Eternity's sunrise.
—WILLIAM BLAKE

I've been listening to birds a lot lately. Watching them with fresh eyes, too, especially when they take their wee swims in the birdbath outside my door. A little water, a little green, a feeder or two, and you too may notice that we are living in an aviary.

In early spring each year, the olive-sided flycatcher arrives. The textbook description of its call is *quick three beers—quick three beers.* But I first heard this three-note melody at Esalen Institute, where we nicknamed it the Be Here Now bird. Early every morning it chants *just be here*, over and over, like an alarm without a snooze button. *Just be here—just be here—just be here—just be here—just be here.* Ram Dass and Aldous Huxley would be pleased.

Mourning doves visit too, filling the forest with their melancholy crooning. Redwing blackbirds trill beside ponds and streams, while acorn woodpeckers, wearing sporty red berets, laugh with each other in the oaks.

In the dawn chorus, the northern flicker calls out *kyeeer,* followed by a rapid-fire drum solo on a tree trunk, quite the morning wake-up call. There are other members of the flock here as well: from finches and chickadees to owls, hawks, and the unmistakable heavies of the bird world, the ravens, with their throaty barroom croaks.

Yesterday I saw a flash of lemon yellow in a sycamore tree, and a small bird appeared. She flitted, as only a tiny bird can flit, among the branches of the tree, tilting her head up to the sky as she sang a sweet soprano song. Ah, the lesser goldfinch.

From majestic condors with ten-foot wingspans, to gem-like hummingbirds with hearts beating hundreds of times per minute, these angels of the animal world have inspired philosophers, dreamers, and lovers for centuries.

A friend told me once over coffee that one of the best things about sobriety is to wake up and really hear birdsong in the morning. Thank you dear friend whose smile I'll always remember. Your words are with me still.

Missing the Goaties

It's funny how ten years ago can seem a different lifetime. What happens to us each decade? What skin do we shed, how do we re-grow ourselves, and into what? We are unraveling mysteries, always.

Two decades ago we raised goats on the mountain. It began when our perpetually barefoot and dread-locked friend showed up one afternoon with an entire flock crammed under the camper shell of his pickup truck. We suddenly had a family of three nanny goats and over a dozen kids.

When I learned how to milk the nannies I sensed my ancestors smiling down on me. Yes, I'm going to firmly grasp the teats of this unwitting farm animal and pull down *hard*, squeezing out streams of warm, smelly milk. It was delightful.

My hands got really strong, as my girlfriend from the city noticed when we held hands months after I became a milkmaid. Milking the goats connected me to people who live closer to the earth, and added a wonderful sense of calm to my morning routine. I even fed my puppy directly from the source, shooting streams of fresh milk into his eager mouth.

We made goat cheese, too, cooking it slowly over the stove or leaving it to turn in large glass jars in the sun. We flavored it with herbs and sold it to the elegant restaurants in the valley.

But milking the goats entailed breeding the goats, since milk production is ostensibly for goat kids, not humans. The babies came and then the milk came. So, we'd invite the billy goat over and avert our eyes. Some months later, if we were in the manger at the right moment, we'd attend to the nannies in labor. With quiet concentration, they delivered their kids calmly in the straw, their only noise a resounding bleat at the moment of birth.

Mostly, I miss the kids, wobbly-legged, little damp guys, with big eyes and horizontal bars for pupils. We made sure the fresh arrivals stood up to nurse, then we'd leave the nanny Madonnas to rest with their babies. As they grew the kids played nonstop, jumping across hay bales and each other, nibbling on everything in sight.

The hard part was selling the young billy goats for stew meat several months later. We had to: they mature fast and attempt to mate as soon as they can with their sisters, aunties, and moms.

I remember when Captain Fuzzy (we named all of them—Cappuccino, Curious, Bebop, Sigh Happy) began to grow into his adult billy-goat nature—as I milked his mom I looked over to see him in a wide stance, head dropped between his forelegs, peeing with relish on his tummy and face.

He lifted his adorable soft brown head and wrinkled his nose, taking a deep, blissful whiff. Ahhhh. Yeah! A grown up billy, as you might imagine, has a mighty stink. Their urine is their pheremonal cologne, and like a slightly oily Casanova, they love the way they smell.

I was always unable to eat them. My husband encouraged me to think of it as munching on a carrot from our garden. Didn't work. I couldn't enjoy dining on any of our capricious friends.

They weren't particularly disciplined at clearing the poison oak or thistles, either. Despite his advanced age, my neighbor Bob and I often chased them out of his rose garden. He'd scramble after them in his worn, laceless wing-tip shoes, quite goat-like himself.

Then our lives changed again. As we became more occupied with work beyond our home, we dispersed our tribe of goats to local chefs and neighbors. Still, the era of the goaties comes back to me each year, when I wake up on cold spring mornings dreaming of fresh warm milk, and of the peaceful feeling that only a bouncing baby goat can give.

Cricket in the House

In these last days of summer, I'm reminded of another reason, beyond the moon and the stars, that I live in Big Sur: the symphony of crickets that come out on warm evenings to sing.

There's a huge community of serenading *Gryllidae* in the garden. Like medieval troubadours, they chirp soulfully beneath windows and balconies. It's a nightly dusk-to-dawn orchestra, playing endless variations on a primal tune.

They harmonize beautifully. One group chants two notes in a seesaw melody, while the other group offers up a long, low hum. They chant a mesmerizing lullaby, perfect for sleeping under the stars.

A tribe of them thrives in the passionflower vine that forms an arch at the entrance to the garden.

At night we stand beneath the curtains of vines and scarlet blooms as the crickets give us an intimate performance in surround sound.

Recently I cut some long strands of passionflowers and put them in a vase above my bed. Later that night I woke to the shrill singing of a lonely green bug right beside my head. It's considered auspicious to have a cricket in your house. It means the arrival of an unexpected gift and brings positive energy into the room.

Naturally, I removed the branches of flowers that morning, and set the little guy free.

I did some research on my musical insect friends. And, oh dear, what did I find? I should have known. All those crickets are having sex, or crying out for it, especially at summer's end, before the cold of winter.

The technical term for their music is stridulation. They make it by rubbing their robust right forewings against the ribs on their left forewings: their own built-in violins.

The males make music to attract females and repel other males. First, they sing the seesaw chirp for amorous attention, then the happy hum, broadcasting their postcoital bliss. It's good to know that romance thrives here on the ridge!

What Inspires You Now?

R ecently a friend asked me this stimulating question. Even in Big Sur we need to fuel our cre-
ative spirits by paying attention to what gives us that
spark of excitement, of dreaminess, of love.

As winter approaches and cold seeps into my house
on a Saturday morning, I find that my wood-burning
stove inspires me. I make my bedroom toasty warm
by crumpling paper, stacking kindling and logs, then
torching it all. As I sit back to watch the flames, my
two cats curl up around me and purr their thanks.
Their feline contentment inspires me to dust off my
zafu and meditate.

The many books of wisdom on my shelf whisper to me
to be still. Soon, I will read them slowly, with my orange

highlighter pen, over cups of coffee. The first sip of coffee in the morning inspires me. Sweet, hot java reminds me that my mind is almost always on spin cycle.

Sheepskin beneath my toes under the covers of my bed makes me dream of ancient tribal royalty traveling via caravan across Mongolia. Bells tinkling around my ankles, wrapped in cerulean silk, I dance beneath the enormous skies of the steppes. Or, on the lawn in bright morning light, each emerald blade of grass illuminated by the sunrise.

The sapphire sea, tranquil today, inspires me as it reaches for miles and miles to meet the sky. At sunset, rose-gray cumulus clouds march across the horizon like elephants on parade. Hummingbirds zoom up to pale blue agapanthus petals, seeking nectar. Temple chimes ring in the wind.

My happy dog rolls on his back in fallen leaves and stretches out his hind legs until they tremble. He arches his tummy up to the sun, rolls over and drops his nose down to the earth with a sigh.

In the night sky, filled with crisp winter stars, the portal of the Milky Way opens as the planets hum through the heavens. All of this saturates my soul.

My sister's husky, zany laugh on the phone brings me home to myself and takes me back down the years. But now is better. Now is always better.

The world before me breathes and vibrates with sacred life, more vivid to me than ever before, perhaps because I am simply receiving this vision.

The work of genuinely welcoming this day, and all that it brings, just as we are, right now, constantly inspires me. When I succeed in savoring even the tiniest taste of this moment, contented tears flow from my heart.

Night Blooms

It's 3:00 a.m. again. My body rises up from sleep with an ache that won't go away. Is this yet another reminder of age? Or is there something deeper that leaves my heart pounding as I chew over my latest existential concern? This is something I've experienced since childhood, this wondering about life, and death.

Tonight I look out the window at the full moon, hiding in the branches of the elm tree. I love the moon so much I sometimes wish we could have more than one. Another celestial body would fulfill fantasies of sci-fi fans, and cause more romantic lunacy. Perhaps, though, one moon is enough.

As she rises over the mountain, instead of continuing her climb into the heavens, I imagine her rolling down along the edge of the ridgetop like an enormous egg. When she reaches the sea she cracks open, and luminous moonlight flows over the waves.

Tonight she shines her searchlight silently across the waters. An owl rustles and moans in the elm tree, asking her endless questions.

Big Sur blossoms this time of year. We are ready for warm summer nights filled with music, laughter, and play. Art emerges again as twinkling lights, colorful lanterns, and prayer flags adorn our public and private spaces. Dancers sway in taverns to the music of performers from all over the world.

In the Big Big Big Sur Fashion show, models strut down the catwalk at the Henry Miller Library in extravagant creations of anything but fabric—feathers, bones, ribbons, beads, and more. In my first performance there I wore only artfully arranged pink, white, and yellow paper muffin cups, fishnet stockings, and a lot of attitude.

In her early summer glory, Big Sur is the Mecca I dreamt of before I migrated here. Can't it always be like this? Here, in our bubble of eye-opening culture and natural beauty, we find both comfort and inspiration.

Morning sunshine splashes across the ridges. Baby quail, like tiny wind-up toys, scurry after their parents across dirt roads. Royal blue and tangerine koi jump in the pond, bright-purple iris appear in the forest. Walking barefoot feels natural again, and— dare I say it?—the joy of being buck-naked in the great outdoors returns.

As I snuggle under soft cotton sheets in my moonlit bed, the night-blooming datura's musky candy scent drifts towards me. Initiates seeking visions call this plant angel's trumpet, and its sticky-sweet golden bells attract the night pollinators. Breathing deeply, I slide back down into dreams.

Ages Pass and Still You Pour

Artist Julia Ingersoll teaches landscape painting in France, Greece, Italy, Bali, and Big Sur. For her, these few words by Bengali poet Rabindranath Tagore best describe the limitless inspiration she feels as a painter: *Ages pass, and still You pour, and still there's more to fill.* Julia and I met recently at Loma Vista, our local *piazza*.

Back in the 1980s, when I was escaping the city, I remember Loma Vista as a sleepy gas station next door to a tumbling-down plant nursery. On the edge of the garden there was a moss-covered wishing well that held donations for the local fire brigade. Inside the greenhouse, suspended from the rafters, were rows and rows of potted pastel begonias.

The Loma Vista highway sign, like a church sermon marquee, spelled out "Gas—Cactus—Beer," in three lines of blocky red plastic letters. I learned later from the gas station attendant, and unofficial town crier, that folks back in the day often asked him for the Cactus Beer.

Now, Loma Vista is the site of a gift shop, a realtor's office and a well-known hip restaurant, but you can still buy gas there and enjoy the view of Mt. Manuel to the north, especially beautiful at dusk.

As we sat at a small table beneath a huge flowering cactus, Julia shared that she'd enjoyed one of those childhoods that seem to create fearless artists. Growing up the daughter of academics with a dose of wanderlust, she attended school in Paris and lived in a village in Morocco.

Coming back to the US, she rode horseback in the shadow of Mt. Shasta and bicycled in the Colorado Rockies. It was, she says, similar to what Big Sur kids experience. "No one told us there were things we couldn't do, so we did everything we could think of—no fear."

After majoring in philosophy at the University of Boulder in Colorado, Julia competed internationally with the US National Mountain Biking Team for almost a decade. After her last race she immediately signed up for a life drawing class in Boulder, apprenticing five to six hours a day with local painters she admired.

Her hard work earned her a spot in the Florence Academy of Art, where she became a self-proclaimed "Italophile" and studied heaps of religious paintings.

"*Madonna con bambino, Madonna con bambino*, over and over," she says with a flourish of her hand, "and in the backgrounds of all these paintings one sees landscapes. The presence of the sacred was a huge part of everyday life in the Renaissance world."

Currently, much of her inspiration comes from the great nineteenth century American painter George Innes. "In his work, instead of characters from sacred mythology imposed on a landscape painting, the sacred emanates from every leaf, shining through nature itself."

Like many Big Sur pilgrims, Julia had no idea she would be starting a new chapter in her life when she visited Esalen Institute (which she has lovingly nicknamed "the butterfly sanctuary") a decade ago. She fell in love there and now makes Big Sur her home base.

Today, when she rides her bike on the Coast Ridge Road, she looks east towards the Ventana Double Cone and west toward the Pacific Ocean. Here she muses on how the ocean is infinity in terms of space, while the mountains are infinity in terms of time.

"The veil between the worlds is very, very thin here," she reports. "Spirit is in all the land, of course, not just in a few sacred spaces. But in places where the land has been abused, spirit retreats. Here in Big Sur, the land pulsates with spirit. Everybody feels it. You can feel your heartbeat in the waves, the soaring of birds—you can't not notice that all life is one."

"All of this is so vivifying," she adds, flashing me her million-dollar smile. "Sometimes I think that being a painter is just an excuse to be out there in IT.

You can't paint what's really there, anyway. It's challenging to be face to face with the ecstatic quality of nature. It can push at the limits of what you can receive."

After our chat, Julia hops on her bike. "Hey, where's your helmet?" I call out, and she smiles that smile back at me. As I head home, I repeat to myself Tagore's poem.

Ages pass
and still You pour
and still there's more
to fill.

Your infinite gifts
come to me
only on these very small
hands of mine.

Ages pass
and still You pour
and still there's more
to fill.
—Rabindranath Tagore

Dansayoga Surprise

This past Saturday morning I took my sleepy self to Dansayoga, a spirited two-hour yoga and improvisational dance class held at the Grange Hall beside the Big Sur River.

There were only the three of us that morning: my friend Diana and me, plus Dansayoga's founder Carlotta, a wild Swedish expatriate who guides us in our dance and yoga adventures. We checked in briefly, complaining a bit about life's ordinary stresses, and, a common theme, the general malaise of mid-life.

Halfway through the yoga class, two angelic, beautiful—and I mean beautiful—shirtless young men joined us from off the road. They gamely formed "planks" and stood with us as "trees." I said a silent prayer of thanks, and tried to catch Diana's eye, but she stayed focused on her poses. Later, I raised an eyebrow and she winked back at me from across the hardwood dance floor.

Yes, these two are exactly the kind of angels we would dream up: with handsome faces, sculpted and lightly tattooed torsos, and a willingness to play. The kind of young man that makes me smile inside, and sigh a little, too.

The energy in the room shifted perceptibly when we began to dance together. First, we moved on our mats, un-kinking our bodies from the hour of yoga. Next, we stood up and began to work through our first self-conscious moves.

Diana, a former professional dancer, inspired me to play with more confidence. The young men dove into the pool as well, ready to cut loose. Carlotta encouraged us to borrow each others' moves, pairing up to follow each other, then switching partners. Everyone dances differently, and mimicry gives a subtle sense of being someone else, for just a moment.

As the music warmed up, so did we, and soon the Grange Hall became the hottest dance club on the coast, all of us stone-cold sober on a Saturday morning. We kicked into overdrive: spinning and leaping around the room, grinning at each other as we tried out all our different moves. The music possessed us as we glowed with the divinity of movement. There's a reason why Carlotta calls this "Dance Church."

As we began to do some contact improvisation, I thought of the old-fashioned traditions of dance, socially acceptable ways to touch and be touched on the dance floor. I saw my shirtless young gentleman in a snappy cowboy shirt, hat, jeans, and boots as we did the two-step together. Couples dancing is deep in the human race, civilized and kind.

Afterwards, we cooled down and sat on the floor in a small circle. Candles glowed on the steps of the stage as we passed around a small, worn book of Rumi poems.

In the stillness after all that dancing, we each read aloud the first poem we found. Then the moment of truth arrived, as it always does. Yes, I had to extend my arm as far away from my body as possible, and squint, in order to read the damn words. Diana didn't even try. When the book came to her she walked to the window, where she read her poem in the brighter light.

Our two visitors were on their hero's journey through Big Sur on a holiday weekend. They confessed they'd never done anything like this before, but had seen the sign on the highway and decided on the spot to join in.

After sincerely thanking Carlotta for creating the space, they quizzed us on the best options for another night's stay. Oh, how I wanted to offer them the hammock in my backyard. But, as I've learned with maturity, fantasy is often better than reality.

As Diana and I left the hall, ready to resume our busy Saturday schedules, our dreamboats stayed behind. "Who dialed up Hunks"R"Us?" Diana asked, and we laughed together under the redwood trees.

Wild Strawberries

Each spring after the rains, we welcome the tiniest little gems of fruit to the garden.

Itty-bitty, they hide under amber leaves and ripen into a dark ruby color. They are tastiest when they're *almost* ready to drop off the stem in sublime maturity. They are unforgettably delicious, especially when served with slightly melted vanilla ice cream and fresh mint leaves.

Typically we harvest only a handful a season, but this year we discovered a bumper crop around the pond, on the path to the meditation deck, and underneath the palm tree.

Searching for them recalls our annual Easter party. On Easter morning we hide beribboned champagne glasses in the garden so our grown-up guests can enjoy the thrill of the hunt, too. Months later we sometimes find a lone, faded goblet in the grass.

You can pick a bunch of berries and marvel at their beauty, but curiously, they don't taste better en masse. So there's more wisdom for you! Less is more with wild strawberries. One, whether plump or microscopic, is enough.

What counts is the explosion of the sun-warmed, juicy essence on your tongue. Succulent and sweet, the strawberry eater's eyes open wide in surprise. Take a moment and savor just one, and you will know the gods live in nature, and their gifts can make us whole.

Jack in the Beanstalk Land

Full tilt fog is back on the mountain. After a week of being enveloped in a moist gray haze, we'd welcome even the stinging insects that visit on hot summer days. All is quiet; even the birds at dawn are mute.

Edges soften and the horizon disappears. Up close, the colors of the garden pop with intensity. We are literally in the clouds as they move up the canyon towards us, to slip through windows and float across the house.

Condensation falls like raindrops from the trees; damp cobwebs shimmer in the grass. Today we can watch a movie, drink hot chocolate, play Scrabble. Yet, we long for the sun.

Yesterday we spent the afternoon *above* the fog as the coast transformed into a mystical archipelago. Wrapped in mists, ridgetops became islands stretching away to the north and south. Miles of cloud banks moved back and forth over the ocean like wooden waves on a Victorian stage.

It's as if someone tucked a fluffy white comforter up close against the cliffs. All we have to do is summon a golden barge and float out on the billowing eiderdown that covers the sea.

The gentleman whose land we live on witnessed this phenomenon and exclaimed, "It's Jack in the Beanstalk Land!"

Yes, we imagine Jack in the branches of a giant beanstalk. The great green stalk sways in the diffuse light of a foggy day as Jack emerges from the clouds to the hillside below our house. Like us, he had no idea what his impulse buy of those mysterious beans would bring, and he's filled with wonder.

Sometimes doing the eccentric thing, like trading a cow for beans or jumping off the merry-go-round of mainstream modern life, can bring unexpected riches. The goose that laid the golden egg, the talking harp, and the giants are all here, living on top of the ridge.

Sleeping Under the Stars

I caught the happy virus last night
When I was out singing beneath the stars
It's incredibly contagious—
So kiss me!
—HAFEZ

These crisp fall nights are magical, with our chirping cricket choir, and balmy breezes tickling the wind chimes. "We should sleep outside tonight," we say, and trundle outside in our fleece-lined boots and cozy robes. Soon we'll be taking down our screen doors, building fires in the stove and putting warm blankets on our indoor bed. Sleeping under the stars will become a memory.

There is a hum in the quiet here, perhaps from the sea, and it soothes our hearts. Under the stars, we can relax in the nurturing embrace of the cosmos.

One of the best things about sleeping outside is waking up at dawn. A ribbon of creamy pink rests all along the horizon, between a cobalt ocean and a pale-turquoise sky. Seen through the floating veil of the mosquito net, this "girdle of Venus" brings magic to the morning.

Doves fly downhill with melodious wingbeats, and a pair of brave crows chase a red-tail hawk away from their nest. Indigo swallows make effortless loops and arcs overhead.

There are restless nights of course, when we inadvertently open the net and mosquitoes bite our fingers and faces. Tiny ace pilots of the wee hours, they alert us to their bombing runs with their high-pitched whines.

A touch of insomnia can be a good thing when you sleep in a planetarium.

The chalkboard smudge of the Milky Way reaches towards the ocean's horizon below us. Filled with mysterious stars, it reaches up and up across the arch of the sky and down to the mountain ridge behind us. We wake to watch it move westward through the night. Sometimes, meteors fall into the sea.

Orion returns this month, emerging from the south flank of the watershed, at around 2:00 a.m. We watch the phases of the moon for optimal sleep quality. A curly-feather new moon is best, rather than a street-lamp full moon that can cause disturbing dreams.

Sleeping outside alone can be a little scary. Sometimes my critters stand guard, watching the wildness of the night with the curiosity of domestic animals. Still, the bed sits on the point of the hill, and is exposed to, well, the entire universe. It would be an ideal landing pad for visitors from outer space.

"Lord, your sea is so vast; my ship is so small," said the seafaring folk of ages ago. The huge mountain rests beneath my bed, while the ocean below sparkles with reflected heavenly light. Reverence comes as millions of planets and stars travel in silence across the endless sky.

Frontier Island

Everything changes. Nothing is forever. Mountains move, rocks slide, roads and bridges collapse. Sometimes, chaos and rubble rule. What we want to believe—that we can count on business as usual—is never true. Security is not just around the corner, but change certainly is.

Maybe this is not so bad. Change can generate possibilities, free us from illusions, and set us on a new path. In adversity we moan, "This, too, shall pass," yet dropping our natural resistance to change can reduce suffering.

In Big Sur, we are a tribe of hermits. Our kinship is in our love of the land. We practice the art of solitude, and do our best to stay grateful despite the anxiety that comes with emergencies.

When the highway closes, a delicious quiet returns to each day. The pace of life slows and we remember. This tranquility is what we came here for, after all. Now we can feel, as our ancestors did, that we are connected to the land, supported by a web of community.

Without traffic (and there's been almost none at all these days due to epic rockslides to the north and south) the highway is hushed, like an empty stadium after a big game. I want to breathe deeply at the vista points, and dance along the tops of the narrow stone walls that stare down at the sea.

The enormous forces that shaped this land are more evident when we're shaken out of our daily routines. We sense the vast, wild seclusion of geologic time. The highway has a secret, hidden when it's busy with tourist traffic. This ever-changing coast is really the edge of the continent. It was here long before us and will be here long after we are gone.

As I drove home last night, my pickup truck was the only beast on the road for a dozen miles. I dimmed the headlights and rock formations became slumbering animals. Pine trees loomed like giants along the asphalt trail. Darkness alternated with flashes of silver light on the sea, stirring memories of when nighttime travel happened only on full moon nights.

If there is a creed in Big Sur, it is that this land teaches, heals, and answers prayers. The Esselen lived here for thousands of years, feasting in forest glades beside streams. Today the soil is rich with their firestones and abalone shells. They had a mystical belief that certain places hold and transmit all that has happened there. All we have to do is touch the earth, and we will remember.

Joy of Stuffed Animals

As the season of giving approaches, I find myself thinking of the most simple gift—a stuffed animal. Children often need to hold something to feel comforted, and to scare away any monsters at night. For many of us, this need remains strong throughout life.

It's acknowledged wisdom that "comfort objects" are an important part of our psychological development. You can make a real difference in the world by giving this kind of toy to a child.

When I was little, I had my friend Bully. He had a furry body and a plastic bull's head, complete with horns. I also had a favorite blanket—a baby-blue quilted number with hot-pink tufts emerging from the center of each sewn square of fabric. Holding these objects gave me comfort. I had long conversations with Bully while curled up in the softness of my blankie at nap time.

I've learned that healthy adult love includes nurturing, hopefully experienced in childhood. Many grown-ups are shy about keeping company with stuffed animals, but they can sure come in handy in times of stress and loneliness. Perhaps if we slept with our personal teddy bears and comfy blankets, more of us would wake up smiling in the morning.

Does the practice of cherishing, of seeing deeply, make our loved ones more real to us? Absolutely. This concept is wonderfully expressed in the classic children's fable, *The Velveteen Rabbit*. The great mystery here is that loving, even loving a fantasy, heals. As Erich Fromm says in *The Art of Loving*, "Love is a power that produces love."

When I gave my neighbor Bob Nash a plush white rabbit during his hospital stay, he understood this intuitively. He missed his cat Teddy, so the drugstore bunny would have to do. He resisted holding it, but when he put it on his lap and petted it, he laughed and relaxed. I believe he connected with his love for life by holding this humble toy, and the process gave him strength.

So, let's nurture ourselves, and each other, by feeling the contentment that only holding and loving can provide.

Spiral of Light

On the cold, quiet evening of the Winter Solstice, we meet beneath the imposing redwoods outside the Grange Hall. We sip hot apple cider from paper cups and await instructions for our annual ritual.

Tonight's ceremony is a way to heal ourselves in this dark time. It's transformative to experience fire as the symbolic guide honored by our ancestors. Like them, we want to welcome the return of the sun.

Many of us have driven down muddy roads through forests to arrive here beside the river. There are several children, one pregnant lady, a few beloved elders, and the rest of us, all in the midst of life. We feel the special energy of this night when the life-giving sun is so far away from our tiny, troubled planet.

We receive a sage blessing, then file into the small dark auditorium in silence, sitting on benches around the edges of the hall. A simple candle glows in the center of the room. As our eyes adjust we see redwood, pine, and cypress branches spiraling outward in a labyrinth that is adorned with antlers, hawk feathers, and abalone shells. The magic of the forest on the floor, waiting.

Our guide begins to sing in an angelic soprano in the darkness. Many of us join in, singing hymns, ballads, and lullabies as all of us, in turn, walk the labyrinth.

As we approach the edge of the spiral we receive a small candle, mounted on a wafer of pine, to light our path. Each fragile flame represents our hopes and dreams for the year to come.

When one person, couple, or family exits the labyrinth, the next enters. At the center, we light our small flames from the amber pillar candle beside the crimson crystal heart. Then we gently place our lights amidst the branches, to shine beside the lights of our neighbors.

Everyone's movement through the spiral is different; some walk with purpose, others stroll thoughtfully, taking their time. Some light their candles with their lover or child; others light their candle alone. For me, this is ceremony at its purest—a pagan enchantment that brings peace.

At the close of the evening, the spiral glows like a two-dimensional Christmas tree, sparkling with the energy of us all. We are quiet together after all that singing, and for several sweet moments the hall fills with shared serenity. The light has returned on this darkest night of the year. Now we move forward with clarity and joy.

Though my soul may set in darkness
it will rise in perfect light.
I have loved the stars too fondly to be fearful
of the night.
—SARAH WILLIAMS

A Friend is Someone Who

"A friend is someone who, while leaving you with all your dignity intact, obliges you to be fully who you are."
—UNKNOWN

I read this on a bookmark that my Uncle Bill gave to me many years ago. At the time I had just returned from a year abroad, and was in a serious culture-shock funk.

There was no café-style night-life in my university town, at least nothing like the expansive boulevards, hidden plazas, and sophisticated clubs of Madrid.

There, I was an incognito American, enjoying *tapas* and *copas* with swarms of Spanish bohemians in the years just after Generalissimo Franco's death.

Back in the US, I joined the ranks of other anxious college seniors on a sprawling urban campus, clueless about what to do after graduation. Uncle Bill offered me a room in his home, rent-free, in exchange for accompanying him to cheap Chinese restaurants in downtown Oakland, and for cleaning up after his cat, PJ.

Every morning I took the bus to the campus from his tiny bungalow, which had been in the family since the 1930s. A former Merchant Marine, Bill had a girlfriend, and occasionally he'd be out all night, a mischievous sparkle in his good eye the following day.

"You should always eat right," he warned, after witnessing my dysfunctional diet of fried food, coffee, and whiskey. Exam time usually put me in a panic, and Bill gave me an anchor, discussing my studies with me. He was the first adult to ask me if I was on track to live up to my potential, encouraging a life-long process of inquiry.

Who can live without friends? Who can grow without love? Friendship can have a sweet, short arc, or become a spiritual ballast for decades.

My friends have taught me how to cook, how to dance, how to love. By example, they've taught me self-love. They've shown me how to laugh when the chips are down, how to work smart, and how to play like nothing else matters. I have met many challenges in my life by receiving the love and wisdom of my amazing friends.

Which brings us to Kipling and Vinnie, my favorite mutts. Two funny guys who have found each other, and who enjoy many shared daily rituals. One a shaggy guy with a big smile, the other a pugnacious "taco terrier." Observing animal friendship invites us to join their world, the eternal present.

Every morning petite and fierce Vinnie trots over from his house to my bedroom door, looking for Kipling. "Time to come out and play!" he says, or, "It's a beautiful morning, let's go for a walk," or, sometimes, simply, "What's for breakfast, dude?"

They'll roll in the grass, wrestle with each other, mark territory everywhere, first one, then the other, and generally have a good time. They're constantly together, and never seem to be bored. Mostly they're quiet, though sometimes Kip diligently patrols the perimeter of the property while Vinnie barks his little-dog head off. These two buddies demonstrate mutual acceptance, companionship and play, essential requirements for any good friendship.

Uncle Bill understood animal friendship, too. He's the only person I've ever known to train a cat. "Make like a prairie dog," Bill would command and PJ would sit up solemnly on his hind legs in exchange for bits of food.

When Bill departed this life without warning a year later, many of his guiding words and kind gestures sank into my soul. There is a beautiful urgency when one soul gives to another, through friendship, this loving permission to be authentic. We find powerful treasures in each other when we are fully who we are.

Sunset Club

At the end of my days, will I simply say that I saw a lot of glorious sunsets? Could this be enough?

When I was a young thing fresh out of college, running wild in the Berkeley hills, I watched sunsets. A group of us met several times a week above the Lawrence Hall of Science to celebrate the sun sinking into the San Francisco Bay. We'd jump-start the evening with a splashy tangerine glow, a different show every night.

Endless combinations of sunsets, constellations, and contrails echoed the life dramas of our small, ever-changing group of friends. We called ourselves the Sunset Club.

One friend from that time, a lovely lost Irishman who came to California by way of Liverpool, had written a trove of poems. One fragment stays in my mind even today, so many years later, written to his former wife:

> To find you
> I came this far
> to where the sun
> sinks into the Pacific
> like an old man
> at a spa.
> —Peter O'Halligan

Now, witnessing the timeless passages of the sun below the horizon has become a lifelong practice, my personal Sunset Club. Yet I ask myself, at nightfall on quiet evenings, is this pleasure, perhaps, too simple?

Sensing the planet turning away from the sun is essentially passive. You have to stop, be present, perhaps enjoy a glass of wine, and express gratitude for the day. There's not a lot of action required to observe nature. Yet cultivating stillness is a major achievement in a world where we all seem more distracted than ever before.

Do I go outside to see celestial bodies at dusk or dawn? Or do I turn to my device for pages of news and gossip? It's a measure of how pervasive contemporary gadgets are that even here in Big Sur we now ask these questions.

These days I find I watch the sunrise as often as the sunset, mysterious but true. A band of rosy-colored sky floats along the horizon above a fog-blanketed sea. This tender display caresses me awake and leads me outside. My feet touch the cool grass. The cats nap on garden chairs. Birds chatter and sing out. Hummingbirds zoom up to the aloe blooms. The day begins.

Then I remember another poem, one of my favorites, from the beloved thirteenth-century Sufi poet:

> The breeze at dawn has secrets to tell you:
> Don't go back to sleep.
> You must ask for what you really want. Don't
> go back to sleep.

People are going back and forth across the
doorsill where the two worlds touch.
The door is round and open. Don't go back
to sleep.
—RUMI

What Would Kipling Do?

It's an odd phenomenon that when friends go away, we find ourselves integrating into our lives the lessons they have shared. It's a kind of psychic sloughing, where special cells merge, and some of their essence lives on in us.

Our animal friends can show us how to live and love with compelling presence. We conveniently forget their painfully brief life spans, even as they bring joy to major chapters in our lives. Ultimately, they teach us how to grieve, and how to let go.

Free of human passions like envy, deceit, avarice, or doubt, unworried by status, or what it all means, they live full and contented lives. Sometimes you can see they are bored or maybe lonely, but they're almost always willing to respond to your attention.

I miss my four-legged friend Kip, a shaggy sweet collie-terrier with vast charisma. I miss him in the mornings when he would go out in the garden and gaze at the ocean, or in the evenings when he would greet me with a big wet kiss. I miss him on long road trips when he'd rest his nose on my forearm as I drove for miles and miles. His soulful eyes are always with me, as is his canine smile.

Once, when arriving at Esalen, to visit the sulfur baths perched above the sea, we were stopped at the entrance by a gate guard who growled that I could come in, "but not the animal."

I looked at Kip in the backseat and I swear he did a double-take as if to say, "Who, me? An animal?" He thought everyone knew he was really a person in a dog suit. The guard peered into the backseat and said with delight, "Oh! It's Kipling," and granted us entry after all.

My goal now is to embody Kip's enthusiasm, simplicity, and trust in life. His ability to drink in the beauty of where we live, his perpetual willingness to play, and his radiant loyalty to those he loved. And Kip loved everyone. Some more than others, of course, but everyone was of interest to him, an opportunity to love and be loved. If he followed you with his eyes, greeted you with a lick, or jumped with joy when you appeared, then you knew you were special.

The mantra I use to keep him close is WWKD? What would Kipling do? And then I must act honorably and simply.

I still see him at the end of the driveway when I come home; in profile, his royal white ruff fanned out below his inclined head. Waiting for me. My most profound hope is that I'll see him again someday. We'll take a lovely stroll to our favorite spot, then sit in the sun on the grass together.

Watching God

This afternoon, long tendrils of fog float across forested canyons, painting a Japanese watercolor against the canvas of the mountain. A spotter plane soars above, moving northwest, looking for sparks from the Soberanes Fire, which now blazes about five miles away from us. It soars up and down the coast nonstop now, a comforting part of the enormous effort to control the wildfire that blasted into our world last week, changing lives once again.

With a bright-orange stripe below its wings, the white plane reminds me of the mango-colored koi in my pond. What will happen to my poor fish should a fire come? During the last blaze, firefighters refilled the pond for them. Hopefully this time the koi will stay safe beneath the pond's cool surface.

How we love our firefighters! They are Earth-wise heroes who do the opposite of what normal humans do in fires. While we may hold the line as long as possible and then run to relative safety, they move towards danger, feel the heat, and outwit the flames.

The valiant fire crews are mostly rural people, some from local indigenous tribes. "We breathe smoke and eat dirt," reported the firefighter who drew overnight duty up here, a welcome break from the Coast Ridge fire line above us.

Can you say "climate change"? So said one of the fire captains, who guided his young team through the danger like a wise bull elk. Yes, we have always had fire and yes, these monster fires are happening more frequently. Today it seems that firefighting has joined yoga and cannabis as a growth industry in California.

As oblivious tourists slip by in a steady stream on the highway below, a bulldozer moves up nearby Torre Canyon. The driver will clear great lanes of dirt on the Coast Ridge Road, creating a barrier that we hope will keep the flames away.

Two days ago I wore a carpenter mask to protect my lungs from smoke. I threw away useless stuff (so much of it!) and took naps between gasps. This past week we weed-whacked the meadow beside the house, hooked up hoses to fire hydrants, ordered fire gel, drew maps, and stored valuables in town. The house has a Zen look, missing many of the works by local artists I've acquired over two decades.

Forget about sleeping well, or pursuing any normal activities with single-mindedness. We sense each breeze, analyze each column of smoke, study topographical maps and Google Earth until we're bleary-eyed. We assertively inform each new batch of firefighters about our water tanks and hydrants, our clearance concerns and exit plans.

It's a "praise-the-lord-and-pass-the-ammunition" moment. We pray to our many gods as the sound of weed-whackers and chain saws fill the air up and down the mountain.

In the universal tradition, I place flowers beneath the statue of Naga, Tibetan Goddess of the Spring, visualizing pure, flowing, sacred rivers. Every evening I light a candle before Mother Mary for protection, and each morning I sing a Sikh song seeking inner wisdom.

It's part of living here—this crazy, impermanent, sand painting life. More than in most places, our community fuses again and again in the crucible of danger.

But this is Big Sur—she-who-comes-up-smiling from destruction—so we count our blessings to be on this roller-coaster ride in nature's war zone.

Today the air is cool, yet each suspicious blast of wind brings dread. As Cal Fire's plane whines overhead heading southeast, the leaves of the elm trees sigh in the wind.

A momentary sirocco makes the neighborhood hawks circle and swoop, upsetting a family of quail who run for cover. Just now, a large flame-colored monarch butterfly swirls up and down, back and forth, against a backdrop of deep blue sea, surfing invisible currents before my eyes.

Last night I read a passage from Zora Neale Hurston's novel, *Their Eyes Were Watching God.* Neighbors are trapped in shacks in the Everglades, in the direct path of a hurricane. As they wait for the storm's arrival, "They seemed to be staring at the dark, but their eyes were watching God."

We watch God here in Big Sur too, a poignant process that shapes our souls.

Liberty Seeds

Nothing in the world
is as soft and yielding as water.
Yet for dissolving the hard and inflexible,
nothing can surpass it.
—LAO TZU

The propane tank is at twenty-five percent, tribes of earthworms are emerging everywhere, and the cat had a seizure. I've stopped bothering to check the rain gauge. While we still have plenty of coffee, rice, and beans, I'm afraid that we may run out of that vital supplement—chocolate.

It's been a rough month on top of a crazy year. Five feet of rain—my height—in just two short months. In early January I traveled up to the city, and, on my return, rocks, trees, and mud slid into the Big

Sur Valley, completely shutting down Highway One. I spent a week with friends in Carmel and longed for home despite ongoing, punishing storms.

I was willing to climb with a backpack over the rock-slide at the bottom of the ridge to hide under the covers with my beloved, but decided to be prudent instead.

A month later I was about to head north again, and wisely re-thought the trip after looking at the forecast. On that Sunday, February 12, the Pfeiffer Canyon Bridge was designated as a serious hazard, thanks to the keen observation of the man who lived beneath it. With significant slides to the south as well, the section of Highway One below us is closed to through traffic indefinitely.

These past two weeks we have reveled in being here on the ridge and not on the "other side" despite hardship. One morning we awoke to snow on the mountains and a bright rainbow over the ocean. We've enjoyed candlelight dinners and then gone early to bed, to sleep like little animals in a burrow. Again and again we listened all night long to pounding rain and howling winds, wondering what new slide the morning would bring.

It feels like we are living at the bottom of an aquarium. Enormous trees toss their branches like kelp fronds and the air burbles and hisses with wetness. The frogs are delirious, croaking endless harmonies in the pond.

Last night we dined on sardines with wasabi sauce, served with a flair as "poor man's sushi." We've found the time to read, to think, to do yoga in the intermittent sunshine. I've opened Joseph Campbell's *Hero with a Thousand Faces,* again, and find inspiration in every well-crafted phrase.

We're looking at several months to a year of difficult crossings out of Big Sur to the North. The exit South is un-traversable until a nail-soil wall is drilled into place, the Old Coast Road is a river, and the Nacimiento-Ferguson road over the Santa Lucia Mountains is crumbling.

It's as if Mama Big Sur stomped her foot, took down her hair and did a full-body shimmy for weeks, saying, "Enough is enough!" She has reclaimed her territory, ending the torrential flow of tourists for a time. Perhaps she got tired of staying in shape for the whole world, and decided instead to give us a taste of her slippery, scary, wild self.

Now, as the storm cycle subdues a little, and the highway is silent, we feel her calm out-breath. While repairs are promised "soon," some of us are discreetly enjoying the quiet. We celebrate solitude and the re-awakening of nature all around us. The whales swim closer to the shore, quail and bobcats wander across roads. When the rains stop, the birds sing.

Systems are falling into place, too. My gray kitty Pearl had a bizarre seizure. This taught me that trying to subdue an animal that is frothing at the mouth with my bare hands is not a good idea. After sustaining kitty stigmata in my right palm, I called our local health center.

To my immense relief the center's resourceful doctor put antibiotics on a helicopter headed down the coast that afternoon. I picked it up from the pilot, who smiled at me and waved the brown paper bag holding the drugs when he landed on the helipad. It was a movie-worthy moment. (Note to self, next job: helicopter pilot?)

Restaurants and inns south of the bridge are currently closed, with the local deli heroically supplying the community with eggs, milk, bread, and beer over a hiking trail. On Valentine's Day, we had one of the last ambrosia burgers Nepenthe will be serving for a while. This iconic spot was nearly empty, with a stream of local lovers showing up to celebrate and enjoy the view.

Many of us blessed to live between mile marker 29 and 45.5 have stocked our pantries in preparation for this kind of event. A bit of a doomsday perspective has helped, as do vegetable gardens, of course.

We slid under the wire on this one, as we acquired twenty cubic feet of dirt a week ago, filling our little truck. Just before we crossed Pfeiffer Canyon Bridge, already beginning to look like a roller coaster, we were informed that there would be no more traffic on it of any kind, ever. We felt like trapeze artists as we drove carefully across the middle of the sinking span in a lane marked by orange traffic cones.

Driving down the rocky coast in the sunshine that day, we saw a painter friend at her easel on the highway, five hundred feet above a cove filled with barking sea lions. While some folks now hike and ride horses on the highway, she informed us that a young woman, completely naked, had just sailed past her on a skateboard.

Today blessed sunshine returns; the lights go on when you flip the switches, the washer and dryer are doing their important work. Outside I pull up large swaths of tenacious scotch broom, freeing invasive roots from rocky soil that has become a buttery clay from the rains.

Some time ago we bought several cans of "Liberty Seeds." We have beets, cucumbers, corn, lettuce, kale, spinach, carrots, onions, peppers, and more—all in super-compact, not-yet-germinated form.

As soon as the rain stops for a few days and it gets a bit warmer, we're going to put dirt into large pots and sow these mysterious seeds. It's a miracle that something so tiny will create a plant that we can eat in the months to come, and we are hopeful.

We're on a kind of frontier now, where communication, patience and self-reliance are all crucial. Simple seeds can provide freedom in the midst of chaos. We're looking forward to a sumptuous Victory Garden, more needed now than ever.

Another Thing I Love about this Town

There's something profound about living in a place that draws people to gather on the edges of cliffs and gaze across the ocean with a kind of longing. It helps to remember this when tourism resumes epic proportions in Big Sur. Inns and restaurants fill up, hikers scale the trails, and the traffic, on both lanes of Highway One, is reminiscent of rush hour in the city.

Like the proverbial lemmings escaping over-population, visitors appear driven by an almost biological urge to come to the coast. As a former city-girl-turned-gypsy who fell in love with Big Sur, I understand. The city is crowded and dangerous, and travelers need a bit of sky.

Our tourists, unlike lemmings, don't actually jump off the cliffs to swim to new territory. Hawaii is a long way west, so visitors remain perched on the tops of cliffs, scanning the view as if looking for important clues.

There's definitely a magnet on that horizon. And those who secretly feel their divine discontent come to this dramatic land to find . . . something. I watch them year-round now. Children jump up and down beside their parents, families pose for group photos, and couples kiss at the precise instant that the sun sinks into the sea.

I've witnessed countless photographic moments that go on to be enshrined on desk or wall: images that record that happy day, that sunset, that kiss. It's an honor to observe people making memories, each one unique, unforgettable.

Hiking up canyons or down streams to beaches, sitting in the sun under the redwoods, taking a bath outdoors, or just gazing at a wildflower, all of this helps us find our way back to the garden.

Then, the stories come. Everyone has a story, and travelers seem to share their lives more easily here.

Something clicks inside, and deeper truths emerge easily, often with surprising humor.

Like most temples, Big Sur is also a confessional. We whisper our secrets to a friend at the sulfur baths, or wail our woes to the heavens from the top of a trail. Years ago, I reread one of my particularly maudlin journal entries as I sat on the warm sand of Pfeiffer Beach. Instead of feeling the familiar twist of grief, I laughed out loud.

Simply observing the vastness of sea and sky from the edge of a vertigo-inspiring cliff produces new perspectives. The eye sees the view, and then, when the mind takes it in shortly after, wordless understanding comes.

Big Sur offers escape, but more than that, it can help us come home to who we really are. Perhaps we can thank our primal, lemming-like instincts for that priceless gift.

The Long Drive Home

Living in Big Sur, you pretty much have to enjoy driving. You also need a reliable vehicle, as every local knows well. There are lots of different strategies for expeditions to the north for groceries, doctor's visits, classes, and social events.

Some folks make infrequent town trips, content to stay home as much as they can. Many make weekly re-supply runs, while road warriors make the trek even more often. Good music, podcasts, and audible books help. Or, just listening to the sound of rubber on the road, which has its own hypnotic power.

Some neighbors go back and forth from Big Sur to the Monterey Peninsula to second homes or studios, creating love nests or artwork spaces. A few rent houses in town so they and their children can skip the pre-dawn school bus stop on the highway.

Others are true nomads, making their living in the world outside Big Sur. They return seasonally to their sanctuaries here, so that, in the words of the poet Robinson Jeffers, they may "touch the earth again."

Each bend in the road has a name, each stretch of highway its special beauty and hazards. There's Old Faithful where the boulders explode down the cliff face after winter storms. There's the curve of the pristine Little Sur River, marked by a cross where a young man drove over the edge, flying four hundred feet down and into the river below. Suicide? Or just late to work? We'll never know.

Cows occasionally cross the road at Lighthouse Flats, and encounters with cattle have become an in-joke for alcohol-induced rollovers. "I swerved to avoid a cow." Wink, wink.

Once a week or so, energized by my evening dance class and my car well stocked with groceries, I follow the winding road down the coast on the hour-plus drive I sometimes feel I could do by heart.

If only our cars were horse-drawn carriages, we could relax the reins in our laps and let the confident horses take us home. Perhaps the pioneers of long ago traveled this way, but we can be sure that they weren't doing it twice a week, or to take a yoga class.

When there's no other traffic late at night, and moonlight shines on the ocean to my right, I realize that, at this moment, I am the only person on the planet traversing this lonely ribbon of road. As I glide down the coast to my nest, I wonder what all the other souls are up to, and reflect on the soothing solitude of my long drive home.

95505318R00083

Made in the USA
Columbia, SC
11 May 2018